Gone Up In Sm

A Thriller

Georgina Reid

Samuel French – London
New York – Sydney – Toronto – Hollywood

CHARACTERS

Rod Lester
Marian Lester
Shelley
Ann
Eric Bowers
Inspector Hardwick
Walter Bowers*

The action takes place in the Lesters' drawing-room at Crockett's Public School for Girls

ACT I   SCENE 1   Six o'clock on November the fifth
         SCENE 2   Evening, five weeks later

ACT II SCENE 1   Next afternoon
         SCENE 2   Ten minutes later

Time—the present

* This character should appear in your programme but is, in fact, doubled by the same actor playing Eric Bowers

ACT I*

The Lesters' drawing-room at Crockett's Public School for Girls. Six o'clock. November the fifth

It is a pleasant, unpretentious, lived-in sort of room with school photos on the walls and plenty of books in various places. There is a french window, L, with curtains drawn. Below this is a large knee-hole desk with piles of exercise books on it. UL *is a large, high-backed swivel chair and there is a table for drinks against the back wall. There is a door to the hall,* UR, *and a sofa* DR, *with a large box of fireworks on it. There is a shield on the wall with the school motto on it. In the centre of the stage, well back, is a wheelchair in which is seated a life-sized, very realistic guy. If it were not for his pink plastic mask he would look almost human. He wears a battered old hat, a scarf, a dark jacket and trousers, woolly mittens on his hands but no shoes on his feet*

Two schoolgirls in school uniform are standing in silence, gazing at the guy in admiration. They are both about seventeen years old and wear the badge of prefect. They are both well-spoken girls. Ann is rather plain, serious and retiring. Shelley is a pretty, giggly extrovert. They are both holding piles of exercise books

Shelley circles round the guy, observing him from all angles

Shelley Isn't he absolutely fantastic!
Ann Marvellous. Mrs Lester made him.
Shelley She's a clever girl, is our Marian.
Ann Sh! She'll hear you!
Shelley Wherever did she get this dreadful old hat? A jumble sale?
Ann More likely the staff cloakroom.
Shelley That jacket is Mr Lester's. I've seen him wearing it at weekends.
Ann It's awfully tatty and shapeless.
Shelley It never looked shapeless on *him*. He could look sexy in an old sack.
Ann Sh!
Shelley He really is an adorable guy. He's nearly as adorable as Mr Lester. (*She sits on the guy's knee and puts an arm round his neck*) Darling Roddy, why is your face so pink?
Ann Shelley, stop it. Somebody might come in.
Shelley He's blushing. He thinks I'm going to kiss him.
Ann Shelley! Don't!

---

*N.B. Paragraph 3 on page ii of this Acting Edition regarding photocopying and video-recording should be carefully read.

Shelley kisses the guy

Shelley Oh, you gorgeous brute, my heart is pounding with desire. Why are you so unresponsive to my embrace? You do smell funny, my darling. I wonder what you're made of?

Ann I think Mrs Lester said she'd stuffed him with wood shavings from the carpentry room.

Shelley No wonder his lap is a bit lumpy.

Ann Well, get off it, you fool. Someone's coming.

Ann drags Shelley off the guy and she stands up just before the door opens

Roderick Lester enters. He is about thirty-five and is a good-looking, attractive man

Rod Ah, there you are, girls. Sorry to keep you waiting. I was having a second helping of apple pie.

Shelley Oh sir! You won't have room for any of the parkin and toffee apples.

Rod Shelley, I have had many years' experience of these Guy Fawkes' celebrations. I know that while I'm battling with the bangers and wrestling with the rockets, you girls will descend on the food like a swarm of locusts and consume every crumb. So I stoke up in advance. Now, have you brought your essays?

Shelley Yes, sir, I've written four pages.

Rod (*cringing dramatically*) Heaven help me! Four pages of your abominable handwriting to decipher. One would think it was written by a cross-eyed Chinaman. Well, put them at the back of my desk. I've no intention of starting them tonight. Tonight we celebrate. I'm not sure why, are you?

Ann I thought we were celebrating Guy Fawkes trying to blow up the Houses of Parliament.

Rod Oh yes, so he did! And it was a jolly good idea and he deserves eight out of ten for trying. Now—(*he gathers up some different exercise books and hands them over*) you can take back these books for the Lower Fifth. Leave them in my classroom, and at half-past six you can come back and get Laughing Boy. (*He indicates the guy*)

Shelley Oh, he's really too beautiful to burn.

Rod Nonsense. He looks like some elderly relation who has outstayed his welcome. If he sits there much longer, I shall leave home. How many guys are you burning tonight?

Ann At least three, if not more. Jenkins has taken charge of the actual burning and won't let us go near.

Rod The man's drunk with power.

Shelley And that's not all he's drunk with. The cider is flowing freely.

Rod Already? He must have some potent stuff. Don't let me see any of you girls trying any. And remember, there's coffee and hot sausage rolls here, for the prefects, at eight o'clock.

Shelley Yes, sir, thank you.

Rod Now buzz off. You can go through the french windows. It's quicker that way. (*He unlocks the window and lets them out*) And while I think of it, don't let the juniors come anywhere near my box of tricks. Matron has got loads of sparklers and harmless things they can hold in their hands.

The girls go out

(*Calling after them*) And Ann! Keep your eye on those Third Formers! They're all budding delinquents! (*He draws back the curtains, watches them go and remains staring into the darkness*)

After a moment his wife, Marian, comes in and stands behind him holding a tray of toffee apples. She is an attractive woman of thirty-five and in many ways she is the dominant partner

Marian Oh, a rocket! I love rockets. Is it one of ours?

Rod It had better not be. They've been threatened with public expulsion if anyone lights so much as a Bengal match before I get there. *They* think it's a safety precaution, but it's really because I can't bear to miss anything.

Marian You're really just a kid, aren't you?

Rod Am I? And who's been making toffee apples all afternoon as if her life depended on it?

Marian The kitchen is overflowing with them. I've got to start laying things out in here. And then there's the sausage rolls for the prefects' little party afterwards. What d'you bet they'll drop them all over our new Wilton carpet?

Rod And tread them in with their dainty little feet.

Marian Can you clear me a surface on your desk, darling?

Rod (*as he clears the desk*) It's hard to explain the universal appeal of toffee apples. They're sticky to hold, it's impossible to make the first bite, and then they dribble most regrettably down one's chin.

Marian But they *look* so lovely—all glossy and dark and perfect.

Rod (*picking one up by the stick*) The bit I like best is the sort of raft of thin, brittle toffee that they sit on. (*He breaks a piece off and eats it*)

Marian Don't, you beast! Who wants to eat an apple after you've had a go at it?

Rod (*putting it back*) No one will see, in the dark.

Marian You hope. Jenkins has got the floodlights working at last.

Rod (*looking out*) That's a blessing. His language was getting so lurid I was afraid for our girls' tender ears.

Marian (*going out*) Tender ears? You must be joking.

She exits and comes back immediately with another tray of toffee apples

Have no fear for the tender ears of those girls. They may come from the best homes in the country, but they know every swear word in the book.

Rod (*taking the tray*) Ah yes, but they say them with such impeccable diction. (*He puts the tray on the drinks table*)

Marian (*seeing the box of fireworks on the sofa*) Oh! You've opened the box of fireworks! (*She sits and examines them, one by one. They are large and expensive*) Oh Rod, how lovely they are! Look at that Catherine Wheel— as big as a dinner plate! Rockets like torpedoes! Whizzbangs, Whirly-birds,—what's this? Satanic Screamer? Gorgeous! Nero's Nightmare.

Halley's Comet. Giant Sunburst. Who pays for all this extravagance?
Rod The parents, of course.
Marian How wonderful it must be to have money. Did *you* have this sort of thing when you were a child?
Rod My school usually put on a good display. Didn't yours?
Marian Not likely. The Bishop Bruce Secondary Modern didn't run to such things. We saved up our pocket money and had a little do in our back yard, but they were nothing compared with this. Our rockets were feeble little things that barely flew over the fence. Our Roman candles sent up a puff of smoke and two coloured balls and that was all. But we enjoyed ourselves. The sparklers were my favourite. A penny packet of sparklers was sheer magic to me.
Rod It still is, you know. The price has gone up but the magic is still the same. Matron's got a whole pile of them, for the juniors.
Marian Good. I shall go and see if I can scrounge a few.
Rod Where did you learn to make such a beautiful guy?
Marian My mother did that every year. Saved up all our old clothes. I used to help her stuff it with torn newspapers. The kids used to come from all the neighbouring streets to help burn our guy. She taught me to make toffee apples too.
Rod I wish I'd known her.
Marian Yes, you'd have liked her. I wish she could have lived to see this place. To see her daughter's husband, teaching at one of the finest public schools in the land. She'd have liked that. (*She pauses shyly*) I hope I don't let you down, Rod.
Rod Let me down?
Marian I'm not out of the same drawer as these girls. Sometimes I feel very conscious of my working class background.
Rod (*moving the guy and chair into the corner of the room*) Nonsense. You couldn't let me down if you tried. You're my idea of the perfect wife. You have beauty, brains and character, and without you I'm a lost soul crying in the wilderness.
Marian D'you mean it?
Rod Every word. I thought you knew.
Marian No. I thought it was just animal passion.
Rod Well, there's that too.

He begins to kiss her with passion but they are interrupted by the door bell

Damn!
Marian Who's that? Are you expecting someone?
Rod I don't think so. November the fifth is a sacred date in *my* diary, as you know.
Marian (*jumping up*) I'll go. You put the fireworks away.

She goes

Rod tidies the fireworks and puts them back in their box

Marian returns with Eric Bowers. He is a rather small, thin man with an unhappy face. He is about forty-five years old. He wears a dark suit and carries neither hat nor outdoor coat

Darling, this is Mr Bowers. He . . . he'd like to have a word with you.

Behind Bower's back she points to her wrist-watch for Rod's benefit, and goes out

Rod (*extending a hand*) Good-evening, Mr Bowers.

Bowers Good-evening. (*He ignores Rod's outstretched hand and goes across to look out of the window*)

Rod I must warn you that I have an important engagement at six-thirty. (*He looks at his watch*) So I can only spare you a quarter of an hour.

Bowers (*unsmilingly*) A quarter of an hour will be sufficient, Mr Lester. You are Mr Lester, I understand? Roderick Lester, the history master?

Rod (*staring*) Yes.

Bowers I wouldn't want to get the wrong man.

Rod Won't you sit down, Mr . . . er . . . Bowers?

Bowers No, thank you. (*He stares out of the window*) The school appears to be floodlit tonight.

Rod Yes. It's all part of the fun. It looks very fine, doesn't it?

Bowers I used to think so. I've always admired the school buildings and I had great faith in the reputation of the school. When my daughter was born, I was determined that she should be educated here. I pictured her, during her formative years, absorbing all the fine old traditions of the school.

Rod And is she a pupil here?

Bowers She was until a few weeks ago. Sophie Bowers. Perhaps you remember her name?

Rod Oh, of course I do. A delightful girl and very keen on history. I haven't seen her since the half-term holiday. Not ill, I hope?

Bowers (*heavily*) Sophie will not be coming back, Mr Lester.

Rod I'm sorry to hear that, Mr Bowers. If you're . . . dissatisfied with her progress, you really ought to see the headmistress.

Bowers No. It's you I want to see, Mr Lester. I've driven all the way from Birmingham on purpose to see you. (*Pause*) What are all those girls doing, hanging around the playground?

Rod Getting ready for the fireworks, of course.

Bowers Ah. Guy Fawkes night. I'd forgotten. It would be better if they didn't see us. (*He draws the curtains across*)

Rod (*staring*) I don't understand you, Mr Bowers.

Bowers No. probably not. But you will. How many men are there on the staff here at Crockett's?

Rod Er—three. Jordan, Shapcott and myself.

Bowers Has it ever struck you, Mr Lester, that when a man takes a teaching post in an all-girls school he puts himself in a rather special position? They are young and full of romantic notions. A man who looks . . . even

reasonably attractive ... must often find himself the focus of their
immature affections.

Rod (*embarrassed*) Of course. It's part of the job that we all come up
against from time to time.

Bowers Do you Mr Lester, do you? And when it happens, do you take
advantage of it?

Rod Of course not.

Bowers Somebody did, Mr Lester. Somebody who my girl admired took
advantage of his position in the vilest possible manner.

Rod Are you saying ... ?

Bowers Yes. I'm saying that last July, one of the masters of this school
seduced my daughter ... had carnal knowledge of my daughter ... on
more than one occasion.

Rod Why, that's ... that's shocking! Sophie should have gone to the
headmistress ... to the matron ...

Bowers Yes, or even to me. But she didn't. She felt, I suppose, a secret thrill
at what seemed to her a full-blown, grown-up affair. She didn't realize
that she was just being *used* by some selfish, randy devil, out for a cheap
lay. (*He turns away*) Dear God, I wish I'd never sent her to boarding
school. But my wife was dead and my work constantly took me abroad. I
thought I was doing the best thing for her.

Rod You say it happened in July?

Bowers Yes. Then school broke up and she didn't see him again for six
weeks. At the end of that time she began to feel rather sick, for the very
good reason that she was pregnant.

Rod (*appalled*) Oh no!

Bowers Why do you sound so astonished? It's the natural consequence of
that sort of behaviour. Nice little girls from decent homes don't dose
themselves with contraceptive pills every morning.

Rod Bowers, this is appalling. How far have things gone? I mean, is it too
late for ... ?

Bowers An abortion? Is that the solution that springs to your mind?
Naturally it sprang to Sophie's too. But because she was frightened ...
terrified ... of what her father would say, she did nothing about it. Just
carried on kidding herself that it couldn't be true. Sitting in corners, day-
dreaming. Telling herself she must be mistaken, God would never let it
happen to *her*. And so she kept her secret to herself until three months
had gone by, and then, in desperation, she went to a backstreet abortionist.

Rod But there was no need for that! Not a clinic in the land would have
refused her a legal abortion.

Bowers No. But she didn't know that. And she was desperate to keep it a
secret from me. So, two weeks ago, at half-term, she crept out of the house
and took a train up to London, found the dingy, seedy address that
someone had scribbled for her on the back of her diary, screwed up her
courage to knock on the door and submit herself to some ghastly
operation at the hands of an ignorant charlatan. And the almost

inevitable consequence was a bad infection which she kept to herself until
it was too late.

Rod (*alarmed*) Too late?

Bowers Yes. Sophie died last week. For the sake of one man's thoughtless
indulgence, my daughter is dead.

Rod drops into a chair, deeply shocked

What do you think should happen to that man, Mr Lester? He hasn't
committed any crime that the law can punish him for. She wasn't even
below the age of consent, so he can't be caught on that score. All he has
done is corrupt and ruin an innocent child and bring about her early
death. What should be the penalty, d'you think?

Rod Why are you asking me?

Bowers Because you are that man, aren't you?

Rod Certainly not. You have no reason to think that I . . .

Bowers I have every reason to think it. Sophie told me.

Rod She told you!

Bowers Before she died she told me everything. How she loved you, how
you passed messages to her, how she used to creep out of the dormitory to
meet you while your wife was away in Scotland. . . .

Rod For heaven's sake, man, keep your voice down.

Bowers You are the man responsible, Lester, and you're no better than a
murderer.

Rod Bowers, for God's sake . . .

Bowers You're not going to get away with it, you devil. The law can't get
you but I can. (*He gets out a gun*) After I've killed you, they can do what
they like with me. Nothing matters now Sophie's dead.

Rod Bowers! No!

Marian enters and stops short with a stifled scream. Bowers turns his head.

*Rod leaps at him and grabs the gun. They struggle, there is a report, Bowers
goes slack and falls behind the sofa. Rod stands up, panting loudly. He kneels
and feels for Bowers' heart, then rises with his hand covered in blood*

Marian Rod! For heaven's sake!

Rod Oh no! God in heaven. No!

Marian He was going to shoot you!

Rod I think he's dead.

Marian But what happened?

Rod He wanted to kill me.

Marian He must have been mad. (*She kneels*) Where's he hit?

Rod Don't touch. It's an awful mess.

Marian I can't feel his pulse. I don't think he's breathing. (*She gets up,
appalled*) Rod, I think you're right. He's dead.

Rod (*in panic*) What are we going to do? What are we going to do? I've
killed him, Marian. I never meant to.

Marian It was self defence. I saw him point the gun at you.

Rod Oh God, what have I done? (*He drops into a chair, head in hands*)

Marian You're shaking like a leaf. Here, let me get you a drink. (*She gets him a small whisky*) My hands are trembling too. Now, we must keep calm, darling.

Rod Keep calm, while there's a corpse lying on our carpet?

Marian Who is he? D'you know him?

Rod He's the father of a girl in the Upper Fifth. Sophie Bowers.

Marian What on earth made him point a gun at you? Was it a joke?

Rod (*bitterly*) A joke! If only it was! He accused me of seducing his daughter.

Marian Seducing? You mean . . . ?

Rod Yes, and the poor kid got pregnant and had a backstreet abortion and . . . last week . . . she died!

Marian Oh no!

Rod And the poor man was mad with grief and before I had a chance to deny the whole thing he pulled out his gun and . . . Marian, for God's sake, believe me . . . I never laid a finger on the girl.

Marian Of course you didn't, darling . . . It must have been some boy from the village. But what on earth are we going to do?

Rod (*rising*) I'm going to ring the police.

Marian No.

Rod (*pausing at the door*) No? Surely we *must*?

Marian Don't rush me. I'm thinking. The man is dead and you, without meaning to, caused his death. That amounts to manslaughter.

Rod I could get a jail sentence! Oh my God, Marian, it would be the end of me!

Marian Yes. Even if you didn't go to jail, it would be the end of your career here. And it's a very sordid little story. The gutter press would have a field day.

Rod That means the school too would be dragged in the mud. Crockett's School with its spotless reputation. We can't let that happen, can we? Marian, I'm stunned and I can't think. Help me. Help me!

Marian Who knows he came here? His wife?

Rod No. He said his wife was dead.

Marian If he set out with murder in mind, the chances are he told no one. So we must shift him as soon as possible.

Rod Yes. Where?

Marian Where did he come from?

Rod I don't know. Yes I do. He said he'd come all the way from Birmingham.

Marian Then we must take him all the way back to Birmingham, find a bit of waste ground and unload him.

Rod I can't. In five minutes time I'm due to start the fireworks display. I could ask Shapcott to take over, "I'm sorry old man but I've got this corpse to dispose of." (*He gives a rather hysterical laugh*)

Marian Shut up Rod. We must stick to our arrangements and act as if nothing had happened. Then later on, when all the fun and games are over, we'll drive through the night to Birmingham.

Rod And in the meantime, he lies here on my drawing-room carpet?

Marian Help, no! The prefects are coming at eight o'clock. They swarm all over the house. You know what they're like. Can we lock him in a bedroom?

Rod Of course we can't. You surely know that there's not a door in the house that has a lock on it.

Marian Well, we've got to get rid of him somehow, without delay. We'd better get the car.

Rod Marian, talk sense. The garage block is surrounded by a seething mass of schoolgirls. The playground is floodlit and I am supposed to be out there, being the life and soul of the party. The headmistress will at any moment appear on her balcony with all the members of the Board of Governors. How can we heave a dead body into the car, right under her nose, and drive it away? It's impossible.

Marian (*her eyes falling on the guy*) No, it's not. We'll dress him up as a guy! Then we'll put him in the wheelchair and while you are keeping everyone's attention on the fireworks, I will wheel him down to the garage and put him inside, chair and all, and leave him locked away until it's safe to move him.

Rod You reckon you'd have the nerve? To wheel him through that throng of girls?

Marian I reckon I could. If anyone asks what I'm doing with him, I'll say ... I'll say I'm giving him to the hospital because the children have no guy and we have several. (*She lifts the guy off the chair and deposits him on the sofa*) Help me lift Mr Bowers.

Rod draws back, trembling

Rod! Pull yourself together. I can't lift him alone.

Together they place Bowers in the wheelchair and turn it away from the audience

Ugh! You've got blood on your sleeve. Good job he's wearing a dark coat so it doesn't show and there's no need to change it. Take off his shoes, darling.

Rod takes Bowers' shoes and puts them beside the sofa. Marian puts the mask on Bowers and then the guy's hat and scarf

Rod (*watching her*) Marian, this is a terrible thing we're doing.

Marian Have you got any better ideas?

Rod No.

Marian Then don't waste time arguing. How does he look?

Rod His hands look too real.

Marian Put the mittens on him.

They get the mittens from the guy and put them on Bowers

I've just thought of something.

Rod What?

Marian He must have come in a car. We shall have to get rid of it. Where did he leave it?

Rod In the car park, presumably.

Marian Which is now full of Governors' cars, parents' cars and all kinds of friends' and relations' cars, so how do we know which is his?

Rod His car keys might tell us. (*He searches Bowers' pockets and brings out his ring of keys*)

Marian What does it say?

Rod "I've seen the lions at Longleat."

Marian A fat lot of help that is. But later on tonight, when everyone has gone home, his car will be the only one left.

Rod Right. I'll drive him to Birmingham in his own car.

Marian And I'll follow behind in ours.

Rod Oh God, I feel sick.

Marian (*wheeling the chair and Bowers into a corner of the room*) This is no time for feeling sick. You hide the guy while I go up and get you another jumper. (*She sees the gun lying on the floor*) Oh, and wipe that gun and put it back in his pocket.

Marian exits

Rod wipes the gun and puts it into Bowers' pocket. He picks up the guy from the sofa

The telephone rings

Rod Damn. That'll be the headmistress.

Still carrying the guy, Rod exits and can be heard talking off-stage

During his speech, Shelley and Ann come in through the curtains

(*Off*) Hallo? Yes Miss Fellowes, nearly ready for kick-off. Yes, it's officially at six-thirty. No, I'll try not to keep the Governors waiting. The programme? Well ... er ... Jenkins will be lighting the bonfire at any moment now. He's not letting the girls have anything to do with that. ... Yes, very wise. It was a rather nasty incident last year and we wouldn't want that to happen again, especially while the Governors are watching. Of course, Jordan and Shapcott will be there ...

Shelley (*seeing the body of Bowers in the wheelchair*) There he is, the precious! Come on darling, we're going for walkies.

Ann Is it all right to take him?

Shelley Yes, Roddy said we could. Pull back that curtain and hold open the french window. Hang on, my hearty, I'm going to bump you down the steps.

They go out, still talking and pushing the wheelchair, and Ann closes the curtains behind them. Girlish voices and laughter can be distantly heard outside

Rod (*off, still on the phone*) ... and then we'll end with a really spectacular burst of rockets and Miss Harding is going to lead a singsong round the fire while the prefects circulate with trays of parkin and toffee apples. Yes, a bit sticky, I agree, but ... well ... tradition, you know. The girls expect it, bless them. (*Pause*) Thank you, Miss Fellowes. I hope your guests will enjoy it.

He puts down the phone and returns, followed by Marian carrying a man's thick jumper and long scarf. Neither of them looks towards the corner where they left the body

The wretched woman wanted to know if there was a printed programme for her visitors! I ask you!

Marian Never mind her. Put on this thick jumper. It'll hide any bloodstains.

Rod struggles into the jumper, but the scarf gets left on the back of the sofa. Marian examines the carpet where the wheelchair and body were previously standing

I hope he hasn't bled on the carpet. Oh Lord, he has! I must get that up at once.

She exits

Rod (*emerging from his enveloping jumper and following her to the door*) Stop worrying about details, Marian.

Marian (*off*) It's an important detail and it's got to be seen to now.

She re-enters with a floor cloth

You seem to forget that a dozen sharp-eyed and inquisitive prefects are due here this evening. (*She kneels and scrubs a patch of carpet*) If I don't get rid of this now, it'll be impossible to shift later on.

Rod (*looking at his watch*) It's half-past six, darling. They're lighting the bonfire. I'll have to go. Miss Fellowes is expecting me.

Marian Yes, you go and start the fireworks. I'll manage the wheelchair ... oh!

They both realize that it is not there

Rod It's gone!

Marian (*jumping up*) How *can* it have gone? It was there when I went upstairs. Where were *you*?

Rod I went into the hall to answer the telephone. You heard me.

Marian Then how could anyone ... ?

Rod It's the girls. Shelley and Ann. I said they could come at six-thirty.

Marian You mean, they came in at the window and walked off with ... a dead body?

Rod They don't know it's a dead body. They think it's a guy.

They stare at each other

Marian The bonfire!

Rod (*rushing to the window*) Quick! We must stop them!

Marian No! (*She runs and gets in front of him*) Leave them alone.

Rod Don't you understand, they're going to burn him! They think he's a guy and they'll put him on the bonfire.
Marian Let them.
Rod Let them? Are you out of your mind? We can't let them burn him.
Marian Why not? He's dead, isn't he? Think, Rod, think! If you go out there now and interfere, the whole story will come out. Every girl in the school is out there. The headmistress and the Board of Governors will have a ringside view of you, grappling with a dead body in the light of the bonfire!
Rod But I can't let them *burn* him, Marian.
Marian Why not? Isn't cremation as good as being left on a Birmingham waste ground? Isn't it better for everyone? Better for him and better for us?
Rod But they'll find out. The girls can't heave him up on to the bonfire.
Marian Jenkins is seeing to that, isn't he? He's as strong as an ox and half sozzled with rough cider.

He hesitates, then tries again

Rod No, Marian, I can't let it happen.
Marian (*vehemently*) You can and you will let it happen, Rod Lester. You and I have been very happy here for five years and I'm not going to throw it over now because some trigger-happy maniac gets himself killed in our drawing-room. I've worked hard as well as you, Rod, helping you in dozens of ways, joining in everything a wife can join in, because I have a dream of one day being a headmaster's wife. I won't allow you to ruin everything. If this comes out, you'll be in the dole queue. You'll *never* get another job. Do you understand that? *Do* you?
Rod (*breathing hard*) Yes.
Marian Good. Then pick up that box of fireworks and go out there and put on the display of a lifetime.
Rod (*looking out*) The bonfire's well alight. There's so much smoke I can't see what's happening.
Marian Then don't look. Simply concentrate on what you're doing. Here. (*She thrusts the box of fireworks into his arms*) Have you got matches?
Rod (*feeling his pocket*) Yes.
Marian (*holding open the window*) Then out you go. Don't let me down, darling. I'll follow you with some toffee apples.

Rod exits, leaving the window open and the curtains back

The glow of the bonfire is visible. Firework effects, from nearby houses, can be seen and heard

Marian takes a tray from the desk, turns off the light and follows Rod, pausing in the open doorway and calling off-stage

Shelley! Have you got a moment to spare?
Shelley (*off*) Yes, Mrs Lester.
Marian Then get another tray of toffee apples, will you? Thanks.

Marian goes out

Almost at once, Shelley comes in at the window with a lighted sparkler*

She crosses the darkened room, switches on the light and puts the dead sparkler in the ashtray. She gets herself a drink, then sees Rod's scarf on the sofa. She picks it up, holds it to her face, inhales and sighs romantically. She wraps it round her and dances a bit, then trips over Bowers' discarded shoes. She puts down the scarf, picks up his shoes, rubs the toe of the left shoe, then fondly places them side by side under the desk. Going back to the table she seems to hear a sound at the window. She swings round, startled

Shelley (*to someone outside the window*) Were you looking for someone? This is Mr Lester's house.

CURTAIN

SCENE 2

The same. Five weeks later. Evening

Rod is sitting at the desk, marking essays. Marian is sitting on the sofa, sewing a man's Elizabethan costume

Rod (*chuckling*) Listen to this. "In November sixteen eighty-eight, William of Orange landed at Brixton." That's Angela Bracegirdle's version. I must ask her what the coast is like at Brixton these days.
Marian Have a heart, Rod. I *always* get Brixton and Brixham muddled up.
Rod Do you realize that William and Mary actually landed on November the fifth?
Marian On Guy Fawkes Day? Fancy that! I wonder if anyone sent up a rocket to remind them.

Rod continues marking

(*After a pause*) Do you think about it much, Rod?
Rod Do I think about what?
Marian *You* know. Bonfire Night.
Rod (*seriously*) Never a day goes by ... and hardly ever a night.
Marian I dream about it, too, but not quite so often as I did. Five weeks have ... blurred the edges a bit.
Rod (*closing his books*) I know. For a long time I went in terror that a policeman would walk in at that door and clap handcuffs on us both. It's only in the past fortnight that I've begun to relax a bit. But even now, a sudden reminder makes me turn to jelly. (*Pause*) I made a fool of myself this afternoon with the Upper Fifth. We were doing Joan of Arc, and I thought I knew what was coming and could face up to it. I was reading aloud from a rather good text book, and I turned the page ... and

---

*NB. Please check with your Fire Officer as to whether a lighted sparkler is permissable. If not then this effect can be omitted.

suddenly there was this picture, full-page, of Joan at the stake, with the flames leaping all round her, and I just dried up and stood there staring at it. It didn't seem to have Joan of Arc's face at all. It had a pink mask and a silly hat. (*He gets up, restlessly*) I got the shakes so badly that I had to sit down and one of the girls asked if I'd like a drink of water. At last I just shut the book and said they could get on with their prep. They all thought I'd gone bananas.

Marian Try not to think about it, dear. It was a ghastly night, but we did the only thing possible. It's over now.

Rod You know, Marian, I never told you this but when we got back from Birmingham that night and you'd gone to bed, I went down in the early morning . . . about half-past six it was and still fairly dark . . . to see if there was . . . anything left. I mean, there'd have to be, wouldn't there? And I found Jenkins had risen early and got there just before me and he'd swept everything up and shovelled it into the boiler room furnace. You know, Marian, I never liked that man, but at that moment I had to restrain myself from giving him a tenner.

There is a burst of laughter from the next room

What's going on in there?

Marian They're trying on their costumes for the school play. I told them they could use the dining-room because there's a big mirror in there . . . and I said I'd prevent you from bursting in on them. Not that they'd mind, I'm sure, if you caught them in a state of undress.

Rod Don't worry. I've had quite enough of adolescent girls for one day. What are you sewing?

Marian Letting out the seams for a rather fat Don Pedro.

Rod You seem to be doing an awful lot of sewing for this play. Isn't anyone else helping you?

Marian Yes, Ann has been a lot of help. She's been making Elizabethan ruffs out of Vilene and they look very good.

Rod What on earth is Vilene?

Marian (*smiling*) You don't really want to know, do you?

Rod No. What I really want to know is . . . how soon do I get my evening cup of coffee?

Marian (*rising*) Right away, my lord and master.

Rod You don't have to drop everything. . . .

Marian That's all right. I'd finished anyway.

Marian exits

Rod goes to the bookcase to choose a book.

After a moment, Shelley comes in, wearing a very pretty Elizabethan costume and carrying a ruff in her hand

Shelley Oh, I thought Mrs Lester was here.

Rod She's in the kitchen.

Shelley I wanted her to fasten this ruff for me. I've tried for five minutes and nearly choked myself. You . . . you couldn't do it for me, I suppose?

Rod I'll try. (*He takes the ruff, stands behind her and strives to fasten it, talking as he does so*) What is it this year, *Romeo and Juliet*?
Shelley Some hopes. It's *Much Ado About Nothing*. I'm the unsullied virgin that all the fuss is about.
Rod You should manage that without any difficulty.
Shelley Yes. Worse luck.
Rod There. I think that's got it.
Shelley Thanks. How do I look? (*She turns coquettishly before him*)
Rod Unsullied as the driven snow.
Shelley It's a pretty dress, isn't it? I wanted the neck a bit lower but your wife said no, it wouldn't be in character. Can you tell I'm not wearing a bra?
Rod Er . . . no. It hadn't struck me.
Shelley It's hellish draughty, I can tell you that, but I didn't want to have straps showing.
Rod Of course not.

The sound of laughter is heard off

You all seem to be enjoying yourselves enormously.
Shelley Oh, it's all right for a change, but it's stupid, really. I mean, all *girls*. Why can't we get some boys from somewhere to take the men's parts? I get no thrill out of fluttering my eyelashes at that great twit, Brenda Fox-Ponsonby.
Rod Mm. Yes, I can see there's . . . something lacking.
Shelley I heard a rumour that we might soon be amalgamated with St Gregory's Boys' School. Do you think there's any truth in it?
Rod I don't know, Shelley. Rumours like that are always floating round. Would you like it to happen?
Shelley You bet. And not just because of the school play, but it would be good for *you*.
Rod Good for me? Whatever d'you mean?
Shelley Well, they might make you Head. You'd make a lovely headmaster. But as long as we're an all-girls school, I reckon they'll insist on a woman for Head, don't you?
Rod There's a lot in what you say, Shelley . . . but it's all speculation. We'll just have to wait and see.
Shelley I shall have left before it happens, anyway. But I would have loved to see you made headmaster, Mr Lester. You're . . . quite the nicest person in this school.
Rod I'd better get you to write me a reference before you leave. Now, shouldn't you go back into the dining-room?
Shelley I suppose so. I really came in to see if you were feeling better.
Rod Better than what?
Shelley Better than this afternoon in the history lesson when you came over all funny.
Rod Oh, that. It was nothing.
Shelley You went terribly white. We thought you were ill.

Rod Sorry to disappoint you. It was just a stab of indigestion. Too much suet pudding for lunch.

Shelley Oh, how unromantic. I was half hoping you would collapse in a faint and then I'd have given you the kiss of life. (*She smiles tantalizingly up at him*)

Neither of them sees that Marian is in the doorway with two cups of coffee on a tray

Rod (*smiling*) The kiss of life? That's an attractive offer. Remind me to collapse in next Tuesday's history lesson.

Shelley (*softly*) There's no need to wait till then. What's wrong with now? (*She reaches up and kisses him fondly on the mouth*)

He stands still, neither encouraging nor discouraging her

Marian enters quickly

Marian That's quite enough, Shelley. If you want to practise first aid, you can practise on the girls. If I catch you kissing my husband again, I shall report you to the headmistress.

Shelley It was only in fun.

Marian No doubt. I just don't happen to like it. Now go back and get changed as quickly as possible and then get back to school. And try to remember that you're a prefect.

Shelley (*subdued*) Yes, Mrs Lester.

Marian Oh, and ask Ann to bring all those ruffs in here and I'll help her sew the fastenings on. It's a dreary job.

Shelley All right.

Shelley exits, a bit deflated

Marian sets the tray down, takes a cup of coffee and sits on the sofa

Rod You were a bit hard on her darling.

Marian What should I have done? Got on with my cup of coffee and said nothing? She'd have had you rolling on the sofa in five minutes.

Rod Nonsense. I'd have repulsed her ... gently ... so as not to hurt her feelings.

Marian Yes, I saw you repulsing her. Standing still and enjoying it. Does this sort of thing happen much?

Rod (*taking his cup of coffee*) Perhaps more often than you realize.

Marian Part of the perks, is it? Perhaps Sophie Bowers tried a bit of first aid, too, and didn't get repulsed soon enough.

Rod (*annoyed*) Maybe she did, but not with *me*.

Marian Well, I hope not, for God knows you had the opportunity.

Rod (*hurt*) Marian!

Marian I'm sorry darling. I've got a nasty suspicious mind. It's because these girls are all so young and ... and blooming and vital. ...

Rod And exhausting. Oh, come on darling, you know what teenagers can be like. You've never let it worry you before. (*He sits in the swivel chair*) Before you came in she said something rather interesting.

Marian Oh yes?

Rod She was saying she'd heard a rumour that we might be amalgamating with St Gregory's.

Marian It's only a rumour though, isn't it?

Rod Perhaps. Perhaps there's more to it, this time. You see, Shelley's father is on the Board of Governors and Shelley reckons that if the two schools combined, they'd be looking for a headmaster, rather than a headmistress.

Marian That's a point. But surely St Gregory's present Head would be the obvious choice?

Rod True . . . only I happen to know that he's already past retirement age.

Marian Is he indeed? That's interesting.

Rod So you see, I must play my cards very carefully and not put a foot out of line.

Marian Oh Rod, if only. . . .

Rod Yes. If only Sophie Bowers had played *her* cards a bit more carefully.

Brief pause

Marian Rod, who do you suppose was really responsible?

Rod Responsible?

Marian Yes, for Sophie Bowers' baby.

Rod God knows. Some boy in the village, I suppose.

Marian I'm not so sure. Those girls are watched over like royalty. Every male who sets foot over the threshold is carefully vetted. Any girl who goes outside the grounds is supposed to have a chaperone. To get into the grounds, a boy would have to climb a ten foot wall with broken glass on top. He'd have to be an awfully determined fellow.

Rod Well, who else is there? Little Shapcott who blushes every time a girl looks at him? Hardly a candidate for a roll in the hay.

Marian Well, Jordan then. He's not shy of girls.

Rod Jordan's not shy of anybody . . . but you know how his wife keeps her beady eye on him. She makes sure that he toes the line.

Marian That only leaves the Bursar.

Rod Good Lord, Marian, the Bursar's got five children already!

Marian (*smiling*) Well, that must mean something, surely?

Rod The Bursar is only interested in his bee-keeping.

Marian Maybe that's just a front. Maybe he lures girls away behind the bee-hives for immoral purposes. (*She stops smiling*) Oh dear, it's wrong to laugh. Poor Sophie.

There is a knock at the door and Ann enters carrying several ruffs. Shelley follows, now dressed in dark slacks and a blazer, carrying a duffel bag

Gracious, Ann, how many ruffs have you made?

Ann Five, so far, Mrs Lester, but I've run out of fasteners.

Marian I've got some upstairs. I'll go and get them.

She exits

Rod Well, sit down then, girls. There's a hard night's sewing ahead of you. How soon is the dress rehearsal?

Ann (*sitting on the sofa*) Just over a week.

Rod Next time they should do a modern play and save you all this dress-making.

Shelley Oh no, don't say that. We love dressing up. Mind you, I'd be glad to get away from Shakespeare.

Ann Oh, no!

Shelley I mean it. There are dozens of good plays we could do, and give the Bard a rest.

Rod Well, what, for instance?

Shelley (*looking straight at him*) We could do *St Joan* for a start.

Rod pauses in mid drink and stares at her, cup in hand

   (*After a moment she continues*) Or what about *The Lady's Not For Burning?*

   Rod's eyes fall. For a moment he sits very still. Then he gets up abruptly, puts his cup on the table and goes out

Ann (*staring after him, perplexed*) Why did he go out so suddenly? What did you say to annoy him?

Shelley I named two plays in which someone is burned alive.

Ann Well, even so. He's a man. Men don't get upset about things like that.

Shelley Don't they? In my opinion there's something fishy going on. Weren't you there this afternoon when Mr Lester had a fit of the shakes? Well, his eyes were glued to a picture of Joan of Arc being burned at the stake.

Ann What are you getting at?

Shelley I don't quite know, but it all harks back to Guy Fawkes Night. Something peculiar happened that night.

Ann Well, what exactly? Stop this vague waffling and be specific.

Shelley I can't for the moment. All I know is, they're frightened, both of them.

Ann Nonsense.

Shelley All right, call it nonsense. We shall see. (*She slumps moodily on to the swivel chair and swings right round so that she is completely hidden*)

Ann I thought it was a particularly nice Guy Fawkes Night. The food was plentiful, the fireworks were good, nobody got hurt, the wretched Third Formers were reasonably well-behaved . . . apart from that little toad who got hold of a jumping cracker and tossed it on to the Head's balcony. That was a moment of rare beauty! The Headmistress seemed to execute a kind of tribal war dance, giving high-pitched squeaks of terror. I know because I was standing right beside her, offering a plate of parkin to the VIP's. Your father was one of them. I'll swear he winked at me, though he was trying hard to keep a straight face. He had three slices of parkin. I hope it didn't upset his digestion. It was as heavy as lead. (*She pauses to drink the dregs of a cup of coffee*)

In the silence Marian comes in with the fasteners

Marian Here we are than. Are we all on our own?

Suddenly the swivel chair turns round. From her duffel bag Shelley has donned a pink mask and an old scarf. She lies slumped and apparently dead. Marian gives a cry of terror, then falls to the ground in a faint

Ann (*who has also had a shock*) Shelley! What the hell are you playing at? (*She runs to kneel by Marian*)

Shelley (*jumping up and removing the mask and scarf*) I told you, didn't I? Has she fainted?

Ann Of course she's fainted. I nearly fainted myself. You ought to be ashamed of yourself.

Shelley I am actually. I didn't think she'd pass out. I only expected a bit of a scream. But it proves I was right, doesn't it?

Ann All it proves is that you're an irresponsible little fool who needs to have her bottom smacked. Give me a cushion for her head.

Shelley does so. Ann rubs Marian's hands

Shelley Is she coming round?

Ann I think so. Her eyelids are fluttering.

Shelley I think I'd better go. I've had two tellings-off already tonight. I'm not in good odour, as the Bard so quaintly puts it.

She exits, taking the mask and scarf

Marian (*moaning*) Oh . . . what happened?

Ann You had a bit of a shock, Mrs Lester, and you fainted.

Marian (*sitting up*) Fainted? How stupid. What made me . . . oh! (*She looks at the swivel chair*) Wasn't there a guy in that chair?

Ann It was Shelley, playing a trick on you. I'm not surprised you fainted. It scared the pants off me.

Marian Why ever did she do it?

Marian gets to her feet with Ann's help and sits on the sofa

Ann I don't know. I gave her the rough side of my tongue, and I'll see that she apologizes tomorrow.

Marian Oh no please . . . I don't want any more scenes. Let's say no more about it. And Ann . . . don't mention it to my husband, either.

Ann If that's what you want, of course I won't.

The doorbell rings

Marian Oh dear, visitors! What a time to pick.

Ann Are you feeling all right, Mrs Lester? Shall I get you a drink?

Marian Yes please. A very small one. Half a glass of sherry would help. I'm sorry that I mustn't offer *you* one too.

Ann No. If Matron smelled alcohol on my breath, I'd be reduced to the ranks without delay. (*She gets a small sherry for Marian*)

Marian Thanks. (*She sips her sherry*) I expect you think it was a bit feeble to faint like that.

Ann It's nothing to be ashamed of. You had a shock. Shelley didn't realize how awful she looked, I'm sure.

Marian No. Probably not.

Ann She's . . . a nice girl, really. She's just a bit headstrong. Often she does silly things and then wishes she'd had more sense.

Marian I was a bit sharp with her, earlier this evening. Maybe she wanted to pay me out.

Ann Oh dear. What Shelley needs is to grow up a bit.

Rod enters with Inspector Hardwick. Rod looks nervous and his eyes flash a warning at Marian

Rod Marian, this is Inspector Hardwick of the Warwickshire Police. He wants to talk to us.

Marian (*rising*) Inspector Hardwick?

Hardwick Good-evening, Mrs Lester.

They shake hands

Marian You . . . want to see us about something?

Hardwick Yes, or rather, somebody. A missing person, in fact.

Marian Oh. Ann, I'm sorry, but this means we can't have our sewing session. Perhaps you could come tomorrow, instead?

Ann Yes, of course I will, Mrs Lester.

Marian You can leave all the things.

Ann Oh. Yes, of course. Good-night, Mrs Lester. I'll slip out this way. It's quicker.

She exits via the french windows

Marian (*motioning towards the swivel chair*) Won't you sit down, Inspector?

Hardwick Thank you. (*He sits on the swivel chair*)

Marian sits on the sofa

Rod You said . . . a missing person?

Hardwick Yes. A Mr Eric Bowers. You'll know his daughter. She attended this school until recently.

Rod Oh, you must mean *Sophie* Bowers.

Hardwick Yes. A tragic affair, I'm sure you'll agree.

Rod Yes. Quite appalling. Do you remember, dear, I told you of Sophie's death?

Marian Yes, I was very shocked. We all were.

Hardwick Sophie had no mother. Apart from her father, her only relation was her uncle, Walter Bowers. It was he who came to the police last week with the information that his brother, Sophie's father, was missing.

Rod That's very strange.

Hardwick Yes. Apparently straight after the funeral he drove off in his car and hasn't been heard of since.

Rod When was this?

Hardwick November the fifth.

Rod Oh yes . . . Guy Fawkes Night. Quite a busy night here.

Marian And he told no one where he was going?

Hardwick Oh yes. He told his brother, Mr Walter Bowers, that he was coming to see *you*, Mr Lester.

Rod Me?

Hardwick His actual words were, "I'm going to Crockett's School to see that bastard, Lester." Did he come to see you, Mr Lester? Perhaps before you answer I should tell you that the lodge-keeper, Jenkins, remembers directing a man to your house at six o'clock on November the fifth.

Rod (*accepting it*) Yes. Bowers did come to see me. He stayed about fifteen minutes and he left before the fireworks began at six-thirty.

Hardwick May I ask what he came to see you about?

Rod He had some idea about donating a scholarship . . . a history scholarship . . . in memory of his daughter. History was her favourite subject.

Hardwick I see. Very praiseworthy. Were you on good terms with Sophie, Mr Lester?

Rod Certainly.

Hardwick I wondered whether you could explain why her father referred to you as a bastard?

Rod I can't. I find it quite incomprehensible. I had never met the man before.

Hardwick Did you meet Mr Bowers, Mrs Lester?

Marian I . . . I opened the door to him. He just said his name was Bowers and he'd like a word with my husband. I ushered him in and left them alone together. I didn't see him again.

Hardwick And you parted on good terms, Mr Lester?

Rod Yes, indeed. He was very cut up, of course. I didn't much like the idea of his driving home in such a state of depression.

Marian Do you think perhaps he had an accident on the way home? I remember Rod saying that he was in no fit state to drive.

Hardwick We've contacted all the hospitals about accident cases, loss of memory, etc. And, in any case, one can rule out the idea of a smash-up since his own car has been found, unscratched, in a back street in Birmingham.

Marian So he got back safely, then? That's a relief.

Hardwick We mustn't jump to conclusions about that.

Marian Surely the car is evidence?

Hardwick Yes, the car is a vital piece of evidence. It's the car that has got us all rather worried, Mrs Lester. You see, someone had gone over every surface and wiped off all the fingerprints.

Rod gapes

Why should anyone want to do that, Mrs Lester? It's not the sort of thing a car owner would do, is it? It makes us wonder if there's a bit of foul play going on.

Marian Yes . . . perhaps he picked up a hitchhiker and got mugged.

Hardwick Mugged, Mrs Lester?

Marian (*embarrassed*) It's an American word. I think it means robbery with violence.

Hardwick I know what it means, madam. It's a very interesting suggestion. Meanwhile, where is Mr Bowers? I should be glad to know of anyone who actually saw him leave this house.

Rod I should think dozens of people saw him. The playground was crowded with schoolgirls.

Hardwick It was dark by then, I imagine.

Rod Yes, but the whole place was floodlit.

Hardwick Well, I wouldn't like to start a mass interrogation of the schoolgirls. Not at this juncture anyway. It would be very bad for the school's reputation.

Rod Have you spoken to the headmistress?

Hardwick Not yet. Do you wish me to?

Rod I very much doubt if she could add anything to my statement. Bowers made it clear he came to see me and me alone.

Hardwick Why?

Rod Why? Well, because it was my affair. The history scholarship, I mean. I'm the senior history master. He said he trusted me to see that it was all arranged in his daughter's memory.

Hardwick And yet he called you a bastard.

Rod So this Walter Bowers says. We have only his word for it.

Hardwick Why should he lie? Is he acquainted with you, Mr Lester?

Rod I'd never even heard of him until you came.

Hardwick Well, there's another little mystery. (*He stands*) But don't worry, we'll get to the root of it. Slow and steady, asking questions, talking to people . . . it always pays off in the end. I must say, this is an intriguing one, though. A man sets off from his daughter's funeral, a man in deep distress, bitter, no doubt, at the thought of a young life ended. He drives a hundred miles to see a man . . . a total stranger . . . he is seen to approach the house . . . and he is never seen again. Disappeared . . . vanished . . . gone up in smoke. (*He goes to the door*) Well, good night, sir . . . madam . . . I'll be in touch again soon. In the meantime, if you could find a witness or two it would help.

He exits

Marian and Rod look at each other

CURTAIN

ACT II

Scene 1

The same. Next afternoon

Bowers' shoes must be placed inconspicuously beside the sofa and Rod's scarf laid on the sofa

Marian is standing alone, unhappily staring out of the window

Rod enters

Rod That was Inspector Hardwick on the phone. He wants to come round straight away.

Marian Oh, no!

Rod He says some important new evidence has turned up.

Marian Something damning, no doubt, and he wants to see our expressions when he trots it out.

Rod It can hardly be worse than when he told me the fingerprints had all been wiped off the car. I could hear my jaw drop with a thud. What on earth made you do such a thing?

Marian I thought it was terribly important to remove all traces.

Rod But you'd worn gloves, you idiot, so you couldn't have left any traces. All you achieved was to get rid of Bowers' prints which *belonged* there.

Marian All the same, he can't connect it with us. All we've got to do is stick to our story that he left by car at six-thirty. It's just a question of keeping our nerve.

Rod Yes. Unfortunately my nerve is just about as firm as a plate of jelly. How's yours?

Marian Not much better. The inspector has a way of listening with a friendly smile, and he nods his head and you think you've convinced him, but all the time his innocent little eyes are weighing you up and deciding how much of this cock and bull story to believe. (*She turns away to the window*) What on earth are those two girls doing? They've been hanging around outside for ages.

Rod They're coming in.

Marian (*moving away*) Well, get rid of them. We don't want them here when that wretched policeman comes.

Ann and Shelley come to the window

Rod opens the window

Ann Please Mr Lester, can we speak to you a moment? It's rather important.

Rod Look here, girls, even a mere teacher should be allowed his Saturday afternoons off. Can't it wait till Monday?

Ann Oh no, sir. *Please.* We're both rather worried, you see.

Marian I'm sorry girls, but we have worries of our own.

Ann I know you have, Mrs Lester. That's why we want to speak to you.

Marian What are you talking about?

Shelley It's about Guy Fawkes Night.

Rod (*after a moment*) You'd better come in.

They enter. Shelley has her duffel bag

Rod shuts the window

Sit down.

They sit side by side on the sofa

Now, hurry up. I'm expecting a visitor. Who's going to start?

They look at each other. Shelley nods

Ann Mrs Lester, Shelley should have told you this long ago, instead of dropping stupid hints and acting the goat. I only got the facts out of her this morning. (*She pauses*)

Rod Go on. Make it brief.

Ann Yes sir. Following your instructions we came and got the guy and his wheelchair at six-thirty on the night in question. When we were crossing the playground with it, we saw some girls fighting. They were a couple of juniors, having a really nasty punch-up. We left the guy and rushed off to separate the ... antagonists. One of them had a bleeding nose, so I marched her off to see Matron, leaving Shelley to go back to the guy.

Shelley Only ... it had gone!

Rod What!

Shelley When we got back to the wheelchair it was empty. I assumed some of those wretched Third Formers had pinched it. I know better now, of course.

Marian What d'you mean?

Shelley Oh dear, this is terribly embarrassing. I'd never have guessed, of course, but for what happened later.

Rod What would you never have guessed?

Shelley (*giggling*) Well, that it was really a man dressed up as a guy. He did it to fool us, didn't he? He did it awfully well considering he was ... well ... sozzled.

Rod Sozzled?

Shelley Oh, Mr Lester, I don't mean to be rude about your friend, but I think he was so tipsy that when he'd dressed up and sat in the wheelchair, he just passed out ... and then, later on, the cold air must have revived him and he got up and staggered away.

Ann We thought you ought to know, in case you were thinking he'd been put on the bonfire.

Rod and Marian look at each other. Rod forces a laugh

Rod Oh no, we never thought he'd be *that* stupid. But it fooled you girls, eh? Quite a good joke, wasn't it?

Ann Yes. But I felt sure you'd been worried. And that policeman said someone was missing and I wondered if . . . well, anyway I thought we'd better tell you.

Rod You're a dear, kind-hearted girl and we're very grateful to you. Now you'd better go because our visitor is due.

The girls rise to go

Marian Just a minute. Shelley, you said you'd never have guessed but for what happened later.

Shelley Oh. Yes. Because he came back, you see.

Marian Came back? Here? When?

Shelley It was quite soon after. I was standing about, wondering who had pinched the guy, and I saw Mr Lester come out of that window with the box of fireworks under his arm . . . and then *you* came out with a tray of toffee apples, and you spotted me and asked me to get another tray of toffee apples. Do you remember?

Marian Yes, I remember clearly.

Shelley So I came in here and I . . . I was all alone. . . .

Marian Go on, what did you do?

Shelley Must I tell you everything?

Marian Of course.

She hesitates

Rod (*persuasively*) Shelley, I'd like you to tell us everything you can remember.

Shelley Well, I dare say you won't be surprised to hear that the first thing I did was to get myself a drink. A small one.

Rod Show us.

Shelley Do it? Now?

Rod Yes. Make us see it. A sort of action replay, like they do on television.

Shelley Well, that window was open . . .

Rod opens it

. . . and it was dark outside, but not pitch dark because of the bonfire and the floodlighting.

Outside the window the Lights are lowered

Marian, Rod and Ann withdraw to the sides of the stage, which are darkened

Bonfire and fireworks effects begin, outside the window

Shelley I poured myself a little drink and drank it, feeling rather guilty. (*She picks up an empty glass and mimes a quick drink*) Then I picked up Mr Lester's scarf and acted a bit silly with it. (*She wraps the scarf round her neck and dances with it*) . . . oh, then I tripped over a pair of shoes. I picked them up and put them under the desk . . . (*she puts down the scarf and picks up the shoes and puts them under the desk*) Then I heard a sound outside the french window. I could see this shadow. It gave me quite a fright, but I put on a brave front and said, "Were you looking for someone? This is Mr Lester's house."

A hand is seen, gripping the door frame. Then Eric Bowers appears in the doorway. He can hardly stand. His face is deathly pale and his speech is slurred. No blood shows on his dark suit. It is not difficult to mistake his condition for inebriation. He wears no shoes. He has the mask in his hand

Bowers I want that bastard, Lester.
Shelley (*nervously*) Mr Lester isn't here just now.
Bowers I ... want ... that ... bastard ... Lester.
Shelley (*decidedly frightened*) You'd better come in and wait for him.

Bowers staggers to the chair, dropping the mask. He sprawls, panting, eyes nearly shut. Shelley edges round the back of the chair, hoping to get to the window but he suddenly grabs her wrist. She cries out with shock

Bowers Where are you going?
Shelley To find Mr Lester.
Bowers Yes, bet you are. All the girls are after him, the bastard. I feel awful. Gimme a drink.
Shelley Do you think you should?
Bowers I need a drink. For God's sake get me one.
Shelley (*pouring him a small whisky*) I ought not to be doing this, you know. It's not my whisky.
Bowers (*tossing it back*) Another.
Shelley (*getting it*) Well, all right. But it'll have to be a small one.

He drinks it, then peers at his feet

Bowers I seem to have lost my shoes.
Shelley Oh, I expect you mean these.

She gets his shoes and puts them by his feet. He bends and falls to the floor with a cry

Bowers You'll have to help me. I can't manage.

Shelley puts his shoes on for him

Once again he grabs her and she is frightened

Don't go away. Keep still. Your face keeps coming and going. I hope I'm not going to pass out again.
Shelley So do I. I think you should stay where you are while I fetch help.
Bowers No. I'm beginning to remember now. Nasty scene. I'd better get away before Lester gets back. Help me up. Oh, be careful. I'm in a bad way.

She tries to get him up but they fall down and she is terrified of his clinging hands and his heavy breath in her face. At last he is upright, leaning on the desk

That's right. Better go.

Shelley Where will you go?
Bowers Got a car somewhere.
Shelley I don't think you're fit to drive.
Bowers No. Maybe have a little sleep first.
Shelley That's a good idea.
Bowers Car. Where's my car?
Shelley The car park is just around the corner.

He staggers to the window, heading to the L

(*Calling*) Turn right!

He turns R *and staggers off*

Shelley picks up the mask and puts it in her bag

The Lights come up

Rod (*coming forward*) And that was the last you saw of him?
Shelley Yes. I was rather worried. He was awfully drunk. But I expect he slept it off.
Rod A nasty experience for you, Shelley. You coped very well.
Shelley Ann says I should have told you before, but . . . you know . . . being your friend, I thought it was more discreet to say nothing. About his condition, I mean.
Marian Shelley, where are you planning to go now?
Shelley I really ought to be writing my English essay. It was due in this morning.
Marian You couldn't write it next door in the dining-room, could you? I'd like to think you were on hand if we . . . if we need to ask you some more questions.
Shelley Well, yes . . . I suppose I could.
Marian There's paper and a pen on the sideboard. . . .
Ann I'll stay too, if you like, Shelley. I've a timetable to plan.
Shelley (*bewildered*) Well, all right. But I've told you what happened.
Marian I'll explain later. It could be important.

She ushers them out, closes the door and turns eagerly to Rod

Oh, Rod! Darling! He wasn't dead after all! Oh, thank heaven!

They embrace

How could we be such fools, to mistake concussion for death! But he didn't seem to be breathing and I couldn't feel his pulse. Wasn't that strange? Oh Rod, the relief is indescribable. (*She stares at him*) Darling, why are you looking so grim?
Rod He's still missing, Marian.
Marian He's *alive*! Shelley saw him.
Rod Shelley thought he was drunk, but the fact is, he was desperately in need of medical attention and if he didn't get it . . .
Marian Oh! What do you think happened to him?

Rod Well, we know he didn't drive *himself* home. I'd pinched his car keys. Presumably he tried to get into his car, failed and staggered off into the darkness. For all we know he's lying dead in a ditch somewhere.

They stare at each other in dread

In the silence the doorbell rings

The Inspector.

Marian Oh Rod, I'm frightened.

Rod So am I. But never let on, darling. Remember the school motto. "Put on the Armour of Virtue."

He grins and goes out

Marian I think I've got my armour on back to front.

Rod returns with Inspector Hardwick

Hardwick Sorry to trouble you again so soon, Mrs Lester.

Marian Not at all, Inspector.

She sits. He stands

Hardwick What a pleasant room this is. And a very fine carpet, if I may say so. New, is it?

Rod Er . . . yes. Well, only a few months old. Cost more than we could afford, really.

Hardwick Not surprised. I bet you go in mortal dread that something will mark it . . . coffee or blood or some such stain . . . eh? (*He gives it a quick, searching glance*)

Marian We've been lucky. So far.

Hardwick (*looking out of the window*) Ah, now I see the school building in all its beauty. Elizabethan, by the look of it.

Rod Yes. Fifteen eighty.

Hardwick My word, it's impressive. I can see why people pay so much to send their daughters here. Got quite a reputation, too, I believe.

Rod An excellent one.

Hardwick Yes. The sort of place a man would want to *stay*, I imagine.

Rod The sort of place *I* would like to stay, Inspector.

Hardwick Yes. One would do . . . almost anything to stay on here, I should think. (*Pause*) And yet, even in a place like this, there is corruption.

Rod What do you mean?

Hardwick Mr Lester, why did Eric Bowers come here on November the fifth?

Rod I told you. To discuss a history scholarship in honour of his daughter's memory.

Hardwick Mm. It struck me as a bit improbable. Well, hang it, he'd just buried the girl. He surely wouldn't feel like discussing educational charity . . . especially with someone he considered a bastard.

Marian I object to that, Inspector. You have only his brother's version of what he said.

Hardwick Ah yes. One must always beware of reported speech. However, something more concrete has turned up now. Mr Walter Bowers informs me that he has found Sophie's diary.

They go tense

I have not yet seen it myself . . . he is bringing it along later . . . but I am given to understand that it is clear from the diary that Sophie was having an affair with one of the masters of this school.

Marian An "affair"? Surely that's a rather odd expression for a schoolgirl romance.?

Hardwick This was no schoolgirl romance, Mrs Lester. It says they slept together on several occasions, with the result that the girl later found herself to be pregnant.

Marian That's terrible.

Hardwick Yes, I quite agree. A sad state of affairs. And yet, human nature being what it is, an all too likely situation. It seems to me that the father of that girl might well decide, as he stood by her grave, that the time had come to face the man responsible. And he might well call him a bastard.

Rod Inspector, I was not responsible. I never touched the girl.

Hardwick Mr Lester, have you got a gun?

Rod I . . . no.

Hardwick Have you ever had a gun?

Rod Yes. Once. I lived for a while in Rhodesia. It was necessary for self-protection.

Hardwick Where is it now?

Rod I've no idea.

Hardwick You see Mr Lester, it strikes me that if a man with a grievance came here one night and threatened to expose you as having corrupted his daughter, you might be very worried indeed. You might so fear the loss of your job at this highly desirable and expensive school, that you would whip out your gun in order to shut his lying mouth.

Rod I wouldn't be such a fool. Shoot a man in a house surrounded by schoolgirls?

Hardwick Ah, but it was Guy Fawkes Night. What is one more bang among so many?

Marian Inspector Hardwick, your idea is sheer imagination. I can assure you that Eric Bowers left this house of his own free will and I have a witness who can vouch for it.

Hardwick Ah! Now that's very interesting. Who is this witness you have managed to dig up?

Marian She's one of the prefects. Her father is on the Board of Governors. You can believe what she says.

Hardwick Good. Can you get hold of her?

Rod She's in the next room. But, Inspector, I do beg you not to say anything to her about . . . about Sophie. They know that she's dead and that is all.

Hardwick I shall be very careful, Mr Lester. You can trust me to be discreet.

Rod goes out

How long have you and your husband been here at Crockett's Mrs Lester?

Marian Five years.

Hardwick You are not, yourself, a teacher?

Marian No. But I take part in many aspects of school life. I get to know the girls quite well.

Hardwick And what sort of a girl was Sophie Bowers?

Marian (*after a moment*) She was a bit of an enigma, really. Very quiet . . . but not from shyness, I'm sure. She always seemed to be watching and smiling to herself.

Hardwick Good-looking?

Marian Very.

Hardwick Are you surprised to learn that she was . . . on intimate terms . . . with one of the masters?

Marian I . . . I could believe it of *her*. But I can't bring myself to believe that . . . that one of *them*. . . .

Hardwick No. It seems unthinkable at first, doesn't it?

Rod comes in with Shelley

Rod This is Michelle Courteney, Inspector. Shelley, this is Inspector Hardwick.

Hardwick Won't you sit down, Miss Courteney?

Shelley sits

I just want to ask you a few questions, if you don't mind. It's about a Mr Eric Bowers who seems to have completely disappeared. Almost the last person to see him, that we know of, was Mr Lester here. Bowers came to see Mr Lester five weeks ago. It was in fact on November the fifth. I expect you can remember that night, eh? Plenty going on, no doubt?

Shelley Yes. There was a firework display. Mr Lester was in charge of it.

Hardwick Is that so? Not the best time to receive a visitor, eh, Mr Lester?

Rod No. But luckily he didn't stay long. He was gone before six-thirty and I was able to go and start the fireworks.

Hardwick And when did Miss Courteney see him?

Marian That was soon after we . . .

Hardwick Please. Let me hear it from Miss Courteney in her own words.

Shelley Mrs Lester asked me to fetch a tray of toffee apples. The french windows were open so I came in that way. I was alone in the room. Mr and Mrs Lester had joined the girls in the playground.

Hardwick (*to Rod*) That would be after Mr Bowers had left?

Rod Yes . . . but it seems he came back.

Hardwick Ah. Go on, Miss Courteney. Why did he come back? Did he say?

Shelley I . . . I think he'd come back for something that he had left behind. I asked him if he'd like to sit down and wait for Mr Lester.

Hardwick And did he?

Shelley Yes, just for a few minutes. He asked me to give him a drink . . . so I did.

Hardwick And then, did you chat?
Shelley Not really. He was so strange. I felt uncomfortable. I was rather glad when he decided not to wait any longer. I directed him to the car park and he left.
Hardwick Why did he need to be directed to the car park?
Shelley (*embarrassed*) He was going out by the window and he went the wrong way. One loses one's bearings in the dark.
Hardwick Of course. And how did he seem when he left?
Shelley Oh, a bit pale, but not bad considering.
Hardwick Considering what?
Shelley (*floundering*) Well . . . you know . . . he'd had a couple of drinks.
Hardwick I see. Would you go so far as to say that he was drunk?
Shelley Oh no! Really, he was all right. Just a bit unsteady, that's all.
Hardwick How many drinks did you give him?
Shelley Only two very small tots of whisky.
Hardwick You saw him take nothing else?
Shelley No, nothing.
Hardwick And the last you saw of him he was proceeding, rather unsteadily, towards the car park?
Shelley (*unhappily*) Yes.
Hardwick Thank you, Miss Courteney. That has been very helpful and I'm much obliged. Don't go away for the time being, will you? I may need you again.

He ushers her out and closes the door

A charming girl and probably reliable. Now . . . we have established that when Bowers left this room he was unsteady on his feet. Did he seem to have been drinking when he arrived, Mrs Lester?
Marian (*warily*) No. He showed no sign of it.
Hardwick And did *you* ply him with drink, Mr Lester?
Rod No. I didn't want to prolong his visit. The headmistress was most insistent that I start the show at six-thirty.
Hardwick Ah yes. Headmistresses are sticklers for punctuality. Now Mr Lester, your witness was very helpful to me but not so helpful to *you*.
Rod What d'you mean?
Hardwick Well, if Bowers took only two small tots of whisky, why was he unsteady on his feet? Do you think perhaps Miss Courteney gave him a lot more than she cared to admit?

They look at him blankly

Unlikely, I would say. She wouldn't make free with someone else's whisky, would she? Yet Bowers was pale and unsteady. He'd lost his bearings. Might it not be that he was suffering, not from drink, but from some act of violence?
Rod That's ridiculous.
Hardwick Is it, Mr Lester? Is it really so unlikely? Consider the facts that we know. Bowers was in a state of grief and bitterness . . . right. Not likely to behave in a rational manner. He came here to accuse you of a very nasty

offence against his daughter. He probably shouted and threatened. If you were guilty, or even if you were innocent, I can well imagine you taking some violent action to shut him up. Where *is* your gun, by the way? And suppose in the struggle, he escaped, and you thought he'd gone for good, but he came back for something that he'd dropped and then staggered off again. Aren't you worried what may have happened to him? Suppose he had concussion? Suppose he was bleeding?

Rod Shelley saw no blood. . . .

Hardwick Internally, perhaps. Aren't you afraid that his body may even now be lying face downwards in a corner of an empty field, or some remote barn where he crept for refuge? Cold as a stone? Like his daughter?

Marian Don't! (*She covers her face with her hands and sobs*)

Rod puts his hand on her shoulders, and takes a deep breath

Rod Inspector Hardwick, you've got a few of your facts wrong. I think it's time we told you what *really* happened.

Hardwick (*with grim satisfaction*) Yes. I'm glad you see it that way, Mr Lester.

CURTAIN

SCENE 2

The same. Ten minutes later

Marian, Rod and Hardwick are in much the same positions as at the end of the previous scene

Hardwick But Mrs Lester, surely the best thing was to send for a doctor.

Marian You don't understand, Inspector. We thought he was dead. We were terrified because we thought Rod would be held responsible.

Hardwick He must have been badly concussed. You say he fell heavily and no doubt he hit his head on something. The best thing would have been artificial respiration. However, I should imagine that when you bumped the chair down over the steps, that did the trick. Well . . . then you say you meant to take him to hospital. What prevented you?

Rod We came across two girls having a fight. One of them had a bloody nose and the other had broken her spectacles. It took a few minutes to separate them and find a prefect to take them to the San. When we got back to the wheelchair . . . he'd gone!

Marian I couldn't believe it. He must have come to his senses and staggered off. If only I'd stayed with him.

Hardwick Yes. Well, we can't put the clock back. All we can do is try and trace what happened to him. I must say, though, I don't rate his chances very high.

The doorbell rings

I wonder if you would allow me to answer the door? I took the liberty of asking Mr Walter Bowers to come here with the diary. That must be him.

He goes out

Rod (*moving quickly to Marian*) Darling, I told him as much as I dared and then I used Shelley's story. Did I do right?

Marian Yes, it was a good idea. Thank God you never mentioned the guy. Do you think he believed you?

Rod I don't know. He's very non-commital.

Marian Oh Rod, what a mess we're in.

Rod Hush. They're coming.

Hardwick enters with Walter Bowers. He is in fact Eric Bowers in disguise, tanned and dressed in casual clothes. His hair is different from Eric's and he has a moustache. He carries a gaudy exercise book decorated with ink doodles and labelled "DIARY"

Hardwick Mr Lester . . . Mrs Lester . . . this is Walter Bowers, the brother of the missing man.

Marian Won't you sit down, Mr Bowers?

Walter (*abruptly*) No thank you.

Hardwick Now, Mr Bowers . . . since I spoke to you this morning on the phone, Mr and Mrs Lester have revised their story somewhat. According to Mr Lester, your brother came here and accused him of . . . molesting . . . his daughter . . .

Walter And he had good cause.

Hardwick . . . and then pulled out a gun and threatened him with it.

Walter That's a lie for a start. My brother never owned a gun in his life. He was afraid of them. He wouldn't know how to fire one.

Hardwick Apparently Mr Lester tried to disarm him, there was a struggle and the gun exploded, wounding your brother in the chest. At the same moment they both fell heavily, your brother being underneath so he took the full impact. He was unconscious and bleeding. They placed him in a wheelchair and took him outside, meaning to get him to hospital by car.

Walter Why didn't they phone for an ambulance?

Hardwick Well, they admit they were in a bit of a panic and at the time it seemed important that the school should be kept out of it. Unfortunately, they had to leave him for a few minutes and when they returned he had gone. It is assumed that he recovered consciousness for he was later seen by one of the senior girls, making his way rather unsteadily towards the car park.

Walter Since when he has totally disappeared. It's perfectly obvious, Inspector, that he is dead by now and this man as good as murdered him.

Rod I deny that. Your brother came here intending to murder *me*.

Walter And why should he want to do that, Mr Lester?

Rod He believed that I was responsible for his daughter's death.

Walter Three people were responsible for his daughter's death. One was the man who got her pregnant, one was the person who wrote this address for her on the back of her diary (*he taps the book*) . . . the address of a backstreet abortionist . . . and the third was the clumsy, ignorant quack who performed the operation.

Marian Well, it certainly wasn't my husband who got her pregnant.

Walter Oh really? How are you so sure, Mrs Lester?

Marian He has told me so.

Walter And you believe him? Inspector Hardwick, have I your permission to read certain extracts from this diary, which I found yesterday among Sophie's effects?

Hardwick Why not? I'd be very interested to hear them.

Walter They are not great prose. You won't be impressed by her mastery of words. But, my word, they paint a pretty clear picture of what went on at this school last July. (*He opens the exercise book*) She constantly refers to someone with the initial "R". "July the tenth. When R. returned my history book . . . " there's not much doubt that she means you, Mr Lester . . . "when R. returned my history book, his hand lingered on mine. There seemed to be a message in his eyes."

Marian A silly girl's imagination.

Walter "July the twelfth. Passed R. in the corridor this morning. He caught me up and asked about the swimming sports. Said he's fond of swimming. Said he often goes down late to the baths and swims all alone. Was there a meaning in his words or was it just idle chat?"

Marian You surely don't attach any importance to that kind of incident?

Walter Wait, Mrs Lester. It gets better. "July the fifteenth. Went down to the village for Matron. Walking back up the hill R. overtook me in his car and gave me a lift. Took a different route and stopped in a lonely lane. I had a feeling that he wanted to kiss me. I let him see that I didn't mind if he did. And he did!!! Oh bliss!!! He made me promise to tell no one of our secret." Well Mr Lester, do you recall the incident?

Rod I remember giving her a lift. That's all.

Walter What a convenient memory. See if this rings a bell . . . "July the nineteenth. Haven't seen R. for a week. Rumour has it his wife is away in Scotland. Weather extremely hot. Dormitories unbearable. Think I'll slip out after Lights Out and go for a prowl in my nightie. *Later.* Did so and saw someone was in the swimming baths. I followed silently. It was R. swimming all alone. He saw me and said, "Come on in. What kept you so long?" I quickly pulled off my nightie and slipped in beside him. I was naked and so was he. I could see the scar left by the operation last year. I was frightened when he touched me but he soon made me forget that what we were doing was wrong."

Rod I didn't! Marian, I didn't!

Marian only stares at him

Walter That bit about his scar was pretty conclusive. Appendicitis, was it?

Marian (*in a whisper*) Yes.

Walter "July the twentieth. Went swimming again last night, with R. Shared his towel to dry off and then lay on the grass together and made love. Oh, what ecstasy!"

Rod Marian, you don't believe this, do you?

Walter Oh, I think she does, Mr Lester. It has the ring of truth about it. "July the twenty-third. R.'s wife is coming back tomorrow. Tonight will be a night to remember. Will it be the last time we shall make love? No, I feel sure our love will find a way." What do you think, Mrs Lester? Have you still got blind faith in your husband?

Marian gives a sob, jumps up and runs from the room

Rod Marian! Darling!

Rod runs after her

Walter closes the diary with a look of satisfaction

Hardwick Well Mr Bowers, that was a very interesting document. May I have a look at it?

Walter Of course. (*He hands him the diary*)

Hardwick Where did you find it?

Walter In Sophie's dressing-table drawer.

Hardwick (*examining the cover*) Hm. Just the sort of doodles my daughter draws on her exercise books. You're sure it's Sophie's handwriting?

Walter Whose else could it be? But since you ask . . . yes. I've brought along a birthday card she sent me in May. You can compare them.

Hardwick examines the birthday card and returns it to Walter

Hardwick Are there any other references to Lester?

Walter Only a few. The romance seems to have blossomed rather suddenly in July.

Hardwick Does the diary mention no other man?

Walter Not unless you count Jenkins who told her off for treading on his flower border.

Hardwick She seems to have made only two more entries. "July the twenty-sixth. Breaking up tomorrow. Haven't seen R. for two days except in class. We look at each other across a room full of girls, and try to smile . . . but I believe his heart is aching as much as mine is. Now his wife is at home he doesn't go swimming alone any more. How can I bear the coming holiday? Six whole weeks' separation from my lover." I wonder why she didn't keep up the diary during August?

Walter Oh, I don't think you need to be a psychologist to understand. She came home, her father took her to Spain for a fortnight, then there were the usual outings with friends to the theatre, the skating rink . . . none of it meant anything to her. Only the big romance was of real interest, and that was in abeyance. But I think you'd better read the final entry.

Hardwick "September the first. A fortnight overdue. Never been this late before. Dread to think what could have happened. Wish there was someone I could turn to for advice." (*Pause*) Poor girl. She didn't write any more.

Walter No. I think she must have left it at home when she went back to school last Autumn. It's pretty damning, wouldn't you say?

Hardwick It makes out Lester to be an unprincipled scoundrel . . . but I'm rather sorry for his wife.

Walter When I think of a man like that, surrounded by innocent school-girls. . . .

Hardwick Well, she didn't sound all that innocent to me. However, that's not my concern. Finding your brother is my first priority, and deciding whose finger was on the trigger.

Walter My brother had no gun.

Hardwick As far as you know.

Walter We were pretty close. I'd have known all right.

Hardwick Lester admits that he has a gun . . . if he can find it.

Walter In that case, don't you think you ought to go after him? He might be destroying the evidence . . . or even making a break for it.

Hardwick (*hesitating*) Perhaps you're right. No harm in keeping an eye on him.

Hardwick exits

Walter pockets the diary, prowls around the room, looks at the drinks but decides against them

After a moment Shelley comes in with two sheets of exercise paper covered in handwriting

Shelley Oh. Excuse me. I came for another pen. Mine has run dry.

Walter (*indicating a jar of pens on the desk*) Help yourself. There seems to be quite a selection.

Shelley Yes. Only most of them seem to be red.

Walter Well, all teachers love red ink. They don't reckon to have earned their salary unless they've written their comments in blood.

Shelley (*smiling*) I think you must be Sophie's uncle.

Walter Well . . . yes, I am. How did you know?

Shelley Oh, the way you speak. And something about your mouth.

Walter You're an observant girl.

Shelley You must be worried about your brother.

Walter Indeed I am. It's five weeks since he disappeared.

Shelley I was the last person to see him in this part of the world.

Walter Were you really?

Shelley Yes. At about a quarter to seven on Guy Fawkes Night, I saw him walk out of that window . . . (*As she turns and gestures towards the window her hand knocks over the jar of pens. They are scattered on the floor*) Ah. Damn. (*She lays her essay on the desk and gets down on hands and knees to collect the pens*)

Idly, Walter looks down at her essay. Something catches his eye. He picks up the papers to study them. Meanwhile Shelley has crawled near his feet and is staring at his shoes

(*Surprised*) Oh!

Walter What's up?

Shelley Your shoes!

Walter What about my shoes?

Shelley rises and stares at his face

Shelley There's a deep scratch on the toe of one of them.
Walter What's so interesting about that?
Shelley But I've seen them before. Your brother was wearing them the night
that he disappeared.
Walter Don't be silly my dear. That's impossible. I assure you these are my
own shoes.
Shelley (*nervously*) Yes, of course. It would be impossible. Excuse me, I
must go.

Bowers quickly gets between Shelley and the door

Walter Why are you so eager to go? Stay and be friendly. I want to talk to
you about my . . . niece.
Shelley You mean your *daughter*, don't you? I'm right, aren't I? You're
Sophie's father who's supposed to be missing.
Walter You're making a mistake, young woman.
Shelley I don't think so. I was here in this room when you staggered out of
that window. You looked very different then, but I'm beginning to
remember. It's not only the shoes that I recognize. There's the voice. And
the teeth. I saw you very closely when I was struggling to get you up on
your feet. You've got a gold-capped tooth on the upper right-hand side!

Bowers closes the door and leans against it. Shelley stares at him, puzzled

What's going on, I'd like to know? Why are you pretending to be missing
and causing all this trouble? Mr and Mrs Lester have been worried to
death.
Walter Your precious Mr Lester has got *cause* to worry. He tried to kill me.
Shelley Oh no!
Walter Oh yes! You thought I was drunk, didn't you? You were wrong. I'd
been shot.
Shelley Shot? With a gun?
Walter Of course with a gun.
Shelley And you want him to think you're dead. You want the police to
arrest him. That's an awful thing to do.
Walter Yes. The world is full of awful things, and as you grow up, young
woman, you'll find out a few more. Are you thinking of telling the police
about this?
Shelley Of course.
Walter Well, I shouldn't. Stop and think if it would be wise. I'm still
holding some of the cards, you know. There's the little matter of this
essay. You did write it yourself, I suppose?
Shelley Of course. What's wrong with it?
Walter About its contents I couldn't say. I'm no judge of the novels of Jane
Austen. She lived in another world where young women were protected.
No, it's the *writing* that interests me. It's very unusual. Very distinctive. I
doubt if there's another girl in the whole school who writes like this. Am I
right?
Shelley I know that it's rotten writing. Why are you harping on it?
Walter Well, it's a funny thing but just as you were recognizing my shoes, I

was recognizing your handwriting. I'd seen it before, you see. (*He holds out Sophie's diary and points to the address written on the back cover*) You wrote that address, didn't you? On the back of Sophie's diary?

Shelley I . . . I don't remember.

Walter Oh, don't waste time. I can see you recognize it. It's the address of a very shady doctor in London who does a quick cheap abortion for girls who are in a fix.

Shelley It was for Sophie's friend who was in trouble . . . someone she knew who was getting desperate.

Walter I'd be interested to know how a girl like you, from a rich home and a sheltered background, comes to have knowledge of such things.

Shelley I don't. Honestly I don't. But I saw it written up on the wall of a public lavatory, and when Sophie said that her friend was desperate, I went back and memorized it.

Walter (*rather sadly*) I see. Yes, it could easily happen that way. Poor Sophie. (*Pause*) Did you ever read Sophie's diary?

Shelley Of course not.

Walter Did it never occur to you that it was Sophie herself who was in trouble.

Shelley (*startled*) Oh, no.

Walter What did they tell you she died of?

Shelley A virus infection.

Walter (*bitterly*) A virus infection. That vague blanket that covers everything and means nothing. Listen to me, girl. Sophie died as a result of having an abortion by the quack doctor you found for her. I told you life was full of awful things, didn't I? When you memorized that address on the lavatory wall, you were consigning her to her death.

Shelley collapses on to the sofa and weeps

That shakes you out of your expensive, well-bred poise, doesn't it? That sheds a light on life that Jane Austen knew nothing about.

Shelley I'm sorry! I'm sorry!

Walter Oh, sorry . . . that's easily said.

Shelley I was trying to help . . .

Walter (*angrily, grabbing Shelley's arm and pulling her to her feet*) You make me sick, smooth little cats like you. You think you know the answer to everything. Now stop blubbering before they come back, take this ugly scrawl you've written and say *nothing* . . . do you hear, *nothing* about me, or I'll make sure that everyone knows your part in the affair. I've no doubt your father is highly respectable. Company director, is he? Do you want him to know what happened? Would your mother be able to hold up her aristocratic head if I were to . . . (*he pauses and listens*) . . . they're coming. Dry your eyes and act natural.

Shelley turns away as Rod enters, followed by Marian and then by Inspector Hardwick

Ah, Inspector. Was he destroying the evidence as we feared?

Hardwick I should imagine that in the last five weeks he has had ample time to destroy any evidence, Mr Bowers. But I would be glad if you would not put words into my mouth. All I can say, officially, is that there is a case to answer and a pressing need to find out what happened to your brother. If you wish to question Mr Lester further, you have my full permission.

Walter I should indeed like to question him further . . .

Rod (*interrupting*) Is it necessary for my wife to be present? It is highly distressing for her.

Walter (*with false gallantry*) I quite agree. The poor lady has undergone more than enough rude shocks for one day. If she would like to withdraw . . . and the other young lady . . .

Marian (*determinedly*) No. I wish to remain. And I'd like Shelley here too. What happened in July is something I have no personal knowledge of and I will discuss it with nobody but my husband. But I *was* part of what happened on November the fifth and so was Shelley, and I am not going to sit weeping in a corner while that man lies and misrepresents the events of that evening. My husband did *not* murder your brother, or even attempt to murder him, though if *I* had been in his shoes I might well have done so.

Rod Marian. . . .

Marian I was brought up in a crowded council flat, Inspector. The original concrete jungle. When Rod and I came to live here I thought I was in heaven. I think I *would* murder to preserve my little bit of heaven. Yes, I *would*. So you can perhaps understand that when Eric Bowers walked in and got himself shot by accident in our house, I was the one who refused to call the police. I was the one who would do nothing when the body in the wheelchair disappeared. I was the one who insisted we drove the man's car to Birmingham. I was the one who wiped it clear of fingerprints. So if you have any more questions, you can address them to *me*, Mr Bowers.

Walter (*half admiringly*) Well, well. Here's a lady to be wary of, eh, Inspector? A force to be reckoned with, not a gentle little housewife with nothing on her mind but toffee apples.

Hardwick I think Mrs Lester would be more discreet if she were to. . . .

Marian Just a minute, Inspector. *What* toffee apples?

Walter (*seeing his mistake*) Surely there were toffee apples?

Marian How do you know?

Rod Yes, how *do* you know?

Walter Obviously . . . the young lady here told me.

Marian Did you Shelley?

Shelley I don't remember. I suppose I must have.

Marian I see. Just for a moment I thought . . .

Hardwick Thought what, Mrs Lester?

Marian There's a remarkable resemblance between this man and the one that disappeared.

Walter Naturally. There's a strong family resemblance.

Hardwick Are you trying to persuade yourself that this is actually Eric Bowers, the missing man?

Walter (*boldly*) Yes, is that what you're trying to say, my dear? It's an

ingenious idea. Your wife's a good fighter, Mr Lester. Better than you
deserve.

Rod Yes. But Inspector, could she be right? It's five weeks since Bowers
disappeared. In that time his wounds could have healed and he could
change his appearance, grow a moustache and then come back here and
try and pin another crime on me.

Walter Such a trick would never fool an astute man like Inspector
Hardwick.

Hardwick I hope not . . . but of course I never saw the original Mr Bowers.
Why don't we ask an impartial observer? Miss Courteney . . . you saw
Eric Bowers on November the fifth. Now look closely at this gentleman
beside you. Could he be the same man?

Shelley forces herself to look at him. She shakes her head

Shelley No.

Marian Are you positive, Shelley? Look carefully.

Shelley (*after a pause*) I never saw him before in my life.

Marian and Rod are very disappointed

Walter (*triumphant*) Thank you, my dear. I hope the Inspector believes you.
And now it's time I was getting on my way. I'll leave the diary with you,
Inspector. If ever a man had a motive to hush up a nasty scandal, this man
has, and I trust that justice will prevail.

Marian Inspector. Before that man walks out of that door, there's something I must do.

They turn and face her

Hardwick Indeed? And what is that?

Marian This. (*She runs to Bowers, lifts both fists and bangs him on the chest*)

Bowers gives a howl of pain and doubles up

Marian (*in triumph*) I thought so! A gunshot wound doesn't heal completely
in five weeks. This *is* Eric Bowers, Inspector. If you doubt it, examine his
chest.

Bowers turns to run but Rod grabs him and forces him down into a chair

Rod By God she's right! It's all a put-up job!

Walter All right, all right, I admit it.

Hardwick You admit that you have wasted my time with a piece of
melodramatic play-acting? Of all the irresponsible . . .

Walter Inspector, before you give vent to any more wrath, let me point out
that *I* was the injured party. I had every cause for resentment . . .

Rod Resentment? I should call it malice.

Walter All right, malice if you like. He tried to kill me, and he damn near
succeeded.

Hardwick I should be glad to know how a man who was so nearly killed
managed to survive.

Walter Well, I was lucky. The bullet hit a rib so it wasn't fatal, just messy and damn painful. No, my trouble was concussion ... and of course shock. Make no mistake, Inspector, when I staggered out of that door I was in a bad way. When I reached the car park, only to find the car locked and my keys stolen, I was at the end of my tether. I've only the vaguest recollection of what happened next. I remember things exploding all around and lights flaring and stars shooting ... and I found myself in the main street outside the gates. A lorry driver nearly ran me down. Luckily I had money on me and he agreed to drive me home and ask no questions. I don't remember the next few days but my housekeeper nursed me and the local doctor patched me up.

Hardwick He was duty bound to report a gunshot wound to the police.

Walter Was he? I don't suppose it lies very heavy on his conscience. I'm a private patient and a generous payer.

Rod Yes, you bought his silence but you won't buy mine. You came here on November the fifth armed with a loaded pistol!

Walter That little tale won't wash. The Inspector knows I had no gun.

Shelley (*loudly and clearly*) Oh yes you had!

They all stare at her

That's what you came back for. I remember it very clearly. You kept wandering round this room saying, "Where's my gun? Where did I leave my gun?" And you found it lying under the table and you put it in your pocket and staggered out.

Walter You bitch! You lying bitch! (*He hurls himself at Shelley, his hands at her throat*)

Hardwick and Rod pull him off, shouting. Marian helps Shelley to a chair

Marian Shelley, are you all right?

Shelley (*taking a few deep breaths*) Yes, I think so.

Rod Get her a drink, darling.

Walter is still in Hardwick's grasp but no longer struggling

Walter That girl's a liar. She's saying it to protect him. She's as bad as he is.

Hardwick That will do, Bowers. It's a lot clearer now, the sort of man you are. That little display of violence shows me just what you're capable of.

Marian But Shelley, why did you say you'd never seen him before?

Shelley Well ... he looked so different. It wasn't until he admitted he was Sophie's father that I saw the resemblance.

Walter She knew all right. She promised not to tell. She was afraid of what I knew about her.

Rod Oh, come on Bowers. A minute ago, she was *my* accomplice ... now she's yours. Hadn't you better shut up before you get in any deeper?

Walter Just you wait till I stand up in court and tell them about you ...

Rod It won't come to court, Mr Bowers. My wife and I will not be preferring any charges. Inspector Hardwick, are you satisfied that it was not my finger on the trigger?

Hardwick That's pretty clear, thanks to this young lady.

Walter That young lady? That two-faced bitch!

Rod Then I'd be glad if you would shift this . . . person . . . out of my house as quickly as possible.

Hardwick Mr Bowers, you're coming along to Birmingham with me to make a signed statement. I shall be in touch with you again, Mr Lester. I suppose I should apologize for subjecting you to interrogation, but when I look at this diary, the apology sticks in my throat. (*He throws the diary on to the desk*) Bowers acted criminally, but God knows he had cause. The whole thing disgusts me. Thank the Lord *my* daughter doesn't go to this school. Good-day, Mrs Lester.

He seizes Bowers and marches him out

Rod Shelley, Shelley, how can I thank you? You lied magnificently. I didn't think you capable.

Shelley I suddenly realized what he was trying to pin on you, and I looked up and saw the school motto staring me in the face. (*She points to the school shield on the wall, with the motto printed underneath it*)

Rod "Put on the Armour of Virtue"? But, you lied. All that stuff about him finding the gun. It was a lie.

Shelley Oh Mr Lester, you'll never know how much virtue it took, to tell that lie.

Rod Well, I'm more grateful than I can say. But Shelley . . . I *didn't* shoot him, you know. It was an accident. You believe that, don't you?

Shelley Of course I do. You're much too nice to go round shooting people. I think I'd better be off now, or I'll be late for tea. Bye!

She goes out of the french window

Rod At least Shelley thinks I'm nice.

Marian (*very quiet and reserved*) Yes. Shelley hasn't read the diary.

Rod I've told you it isn't true. It's a . . . travesty of half-truths. If you loved me, you'd believe me.

Marian Oh Rod, I've watched you, ever since we came to this school. I've watched how the girls react to you, to your good looks, your friendly smile, and your unshakeable courtesy. You're too good to be true. They fall down at your feet like a pack of cards. You can't help it. It hasn't been easy for you, to keep them all at a distance. Shelley's just a case in point. You try, but you can't bear to hurt their feelings. But I always knew that one day there'd be a girl, more attractive than all the rest, more physically alluring, and that you wouldn't be able to resist her. And last July, when I was away, it happened, didn't it?

Rod It wasn't like she said, Marian. I did give her a lift but I didn't kiss her. She did come down to the baths one night, quite uninvited, but I wasn't naked and neither was she.

Marian Then how did she see your scar?

Rod She didn't. I must have mentioned it some time.

Marian Don't go on about it Rod. It's all too painful. I can't bear it.

Rod I see. You won't hear my defence. I'm judged and found guilty. And yet, in spite of that, you fought like a tiger to save me from Bowers. Why?

Marian I can't bear injustice.

Rod And . . . is that all?

Marian No. I was fighting for us. For our life together. You don't stop loving someone, just because they have feet of clay. You just . . . stop respecting them.

Rod I see.

The door opens. Ann comes in with her hands full of ruffs

Ann I'm sorry to burst in but Shelley seems to have gone back to school and I think I'd better go too. I got on with the ruffs while I was waiting, Mrs Lester. They're finished now.

Marian Thank you very much Ann. Put them on the desk.

Ann does so and the diary catches her eye

Ann Oh! That looks just like Sophie Bowers' diary.

Rod Leave it alone! Don't open it!

Ann I don't need to. I know that diary by heart.

Rod and Marian stare at Ann as she moves towards the door

Rod Ann! Don't go. What do you mean, you know that diary by heart?

Ann (*after a moment's thought*) I used to share a room with Sophie Bowers all last year. She . . . she wasn't a very nice girl. I know one shouldn't speak ill of the dead but . . . Sophie was a nymphomaniac. She made no secret of it to me. I think she wanted to shock me. She told me plainly that she intended to "get laid" by every man in the school. And I think she succeeded with most of them. She was very . . . mature, if you know what I mean. But she couldn't get Mr Lester. He had the effrontery to turn her down and she couldn't forgive him. So she used to write the most dreadful lies about him in her diary and read them out to me. She always said she was going to leave it about where the headmistress could find it. Is that what happened?

Rod No Ann. Thank goodness that hasn't happened.

Ann Oh, I'm glad. Have you read it?

Rod Some of it.

Ann Isn't it awful? If I were you I'd burn it, right away. Bye-bye, Mrs Lester. I'll see you at the dress rehearsal.

Ann exits

Marian (*running to Rod*) Forgive me, darling. I should never have suspected you.

Rod Indeed you shouldn't. My armour may have a few dents in it and daylight gets in through the chinks, but I still stagger around in it, for your sake.

Marian You make me feel ashamed.

Rod No, don't be ashamed. You've been wonderful. A tower of strength.

She turns away

What's the matter? What are you crying for?

Marian I don't know. Reaction, I suppose. I can't believe it's all over.

Rod Here, dry those tears. I've got two pieces of news that should cheer you up immensely.

Marian What?

Rod There's a new music master coming next term and he's much better looking than I am and about ten years younger.

Marian (*laughing*) Bless him! He'll oust you from the girls' hearts and become sex symbol number one. You'll be relegated to the second division. How splendid! What's the other piece of news?

Rod The Board of Governors have appointed me Assistant Head. We're on our way up, darling.

Marian Oh Rod!

They embrace

CURTAIN

FURNITURE AND PROPERTY LIST

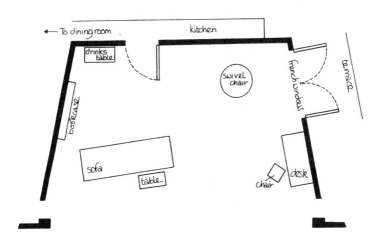

ACT I

Scene 1

On stage: Knee-hole desk. *On it:* 2 piles of exercise books, jar of ball-point pens, various text books, files and papers, ashtray
Large high-backed swivel chair
Drinks table. *On it:* sherry, whisky, glasses
Sofa. *On it:* large box of fireworks, open. *Behind it:* small bowl of stage blood
Coffee table
Bookcase
c stage. Wheelchair containing a life-size guy in dark clothes, mask, old hat, scarf, mittens, no shoes
Shield on the wall with the school motto on it
Curtains open

Off stage: 2 trays of toffee apples **(Marian)**
Pile of exercise books **(Shelley** and **Ann)**
Man's thick jumper and long scarf **(Marian)**

Floor cloth **(Marian)**
Lighted sparkler **(Shelley)**—optional

Personal: **Marian:** wrist-watch
Bowers: gun and key ring in suit pocket
Rod: handkerchief, wrist-watch

SCENE 2

Strike: Mask (place in **Shelley**'s duffel bag), shoes, scarf

Set: Don Pedro's costume on the sofa, needle, thread and scissors on the coffee
table and a pile of essays for Rod to mark on his desk
Curtains closed

Off stage: Tray with coffee pot and two cups and saucers **(Marian)**
Elizabethan ruff **(Shelley)**
5 Elizabethan ruffs **(Ann)**
Duffel bag containing guy's mask and scarf **(Shelley)**
Card of snap fasteners **(Marian)**

ACT II

SCENE I

Strike: Ruffs, Don Pedro's costume and the sewing kit, coffee tray

Set: **Bower**'s shoes and **Rod**'s scarf
Curtains open

Off stage: Empty duffel bag **(Shelley)**
Mask **(Eric Bowers)**

SCENE 2

Curtains open

Strike: **Rod**'s scarf, whisky glass

Off stage: Diary, birthday card **(Walter Bowers)**
Handwritten essay on lined paper **(Shelley)**
Five ruffs **(Ann)**

Personal: **Walter Bowers:** false moustache

LIGHTING PLOT

Property fittings required: nil

Interior. A drawing-room. The same scene throughout

ACT I

To open: Evening. Full general lighting

Cue 1	As **Rod** exits	(Page 12)
	Bonfire glow outside window	
Cue 2	**Marian** turns off the light	(Page 12)
	Lights dim	
Cue 3	**Shelley** switches on the light	(Page 13)
	Lights up	
Cue 4	As Scene 2 opens	(Page 13)
	Evening. Full general lighting	

ACT II

To open: Afternoon. Full general lighting

Cue 5	**Shelley:** ". . . the bonfire and the floodlighting."	(Page 25)
	Lights lowered outside the window. All interior lights down except a spot on C for the flashback. Glow of bonfire and firework flashes outside the window	
Cue 6	**Shelley** picks up the mask and puts it in her bag	(Page 27)
	Bonfire down. Lights up.	
Cue 7	As Scene 2 opens	(Page 32)
	Afternoon. Full general lighting	

EFFECTS PLOT

ACT I

·

Cue 1	As **Rod** kisses **Marian** *Doorbell*	(Page 4)
Cue 2	As **Rod** and **Bowers** struggle *Gun shot*	(Page 7)
Cue 3	As **Rod** picks up the guy from the sofa *Telephone rings*	(Page 10)
Cue 4	**Ann** closes the curtains *Girlish voices and laughter in distance*	
Cue 5	As **Rod** exits *Firework effects*	(Page 12)
Cue 6	**Ann:** ". . . of course I won't." *Doorbell*	(Page 19)

ACT II

Cue 7	As the Lights are lowered *Firework effects*	(Page 25)
Cue 8	As **Rod** and **Marian** stare at each other in dread *Doorbell*	(Page 28)
Cue 9	**Hardwick:** ". . . I don't rate his chances very high." *Doorbell*	(Page 32)

MADE AND PRINTED IN GREAT BRITAIN BY
LATIMER TREND & COMPANY LTD PLYMOUTH

MADE IN ENGLAND